MARK ZUCKERBERG

BY SARA GREEN

BELLWETHER MEDIA • MINNEAPOLIS, MN

Jump into the cockpit and take flight with Pilot books. Your journey will take you on high-energy adventures as you learn about all that is wild, weird, fascinating, and fun!

This edition first published in 2015 by Bellwether Media, Inc.

No part of this publication may be reproduced in whole or in part without written permission of the publisher. For information regarding permission, write to Bellwether Media, Inc., Attention: Permissions Department, 5357 Penn Avenue South, Minneapolis, MN 55419.

Library of Congress Cataloging-in-Publication Data

Green, Sara, 1964- author.
  Mark Zuckerberg / by Sara Green.
     pages cm. – (Pilot. Tech Icons)
  Summary: "Engaging images accompany information about Mark Zuckerberg. The combination of high-interest subject matter and narrative text is intended for students in grades 3 through 7"– Provided by publisher.
  Audience: Ages 7-12.
  Includes bibliographical references and index.
  ISBN 978-1-60014-992-4 (hardcover : alk. paper)
  1. Zuckerberg, Mark, 1984–Juvenile literature. 2. Facebook (Firm)–Juvenile literature. 3. Facebook (Electronic resource)–Juvertile literature. 4. Online social networks–Juvenile literature. 5. Webmasters–United States–Biography–Juvenile literature. 6. Businessmen–United States–Biography–Juvenile literature. I. Title.
  HM743.F33G74 2014
  006.7'54092–dc23
                          2014002740

Printed in the United States of America, North Mankato, MN.

TABLE OF CONTENTS

Like

CHAPTER 1

WHO IS MARK ZUCKERBERG?

Mark Zuckerberg changed how people all over the world connect and share information. He is a **co-founder** of Facebook. The web site is one of the largest **social networks** on Earth. Mark's success as an **entrepreneur** has made him one of the world's youngest billionaires. Today, he is worth more than $25 billion. Mark is also a well-known **philanthropist**.

Mark was born on May 14, 1984, in White Plains, New York. He grew up in the nearby village of Dobbs Ferry. His father, Edward, ran a dental practice connected to the family home. His mother, Karen, is a licensed **psychiatrist**. She managed the dental office and cared for Mark and his sisters. Mark's family always supported his interests growing up.

ICON BIO

Name: Mark Elliot Zuckerberg

Nickname: Zuck

Birthday: May 14, 1984

Hometown: Dobbs Ferry, New York

Marital status: Married to Priscilla Chan since 2012

Hobbies/ Interests: Fencing, traveling

CHAPTER 2

A YOUNG TALENT

From a young age, Mark enjoyed working on computers. His father taught him how to write **computer code** when he was in elementary school. Soon, Mark began to program computer games based on board games. He also created games inspired by his friends' drawings.

Mark's computer skills developed as he grew up. At the age of 12, he created an **instant messaging system** called ZuckNet. Family members used it to send messages to one another at home. Mark's father also used the program in his dental office.

Mark attended his local high school for two years. However, the math and computer classes did not challenge him. Mark's father hired a tutor for Mark. The tutor realized that Mark was not an ordinary student. He was a computer **prodigy**.

READY, SET, ACTION!

As children, Mark and his sister, Randi, wrote and filmed a movie called *The Star Wars Sill-ogy*. It made fun of the *Star Wars* movies.

"I really like making stuff and getting stuff done."
— Mark Zuckerberg

At the beginning of his junior year, Mark transferred to Phillips Exeter Academy in Exeter, New Hampshire. There, classes challenged and interested him. He won academic prizes in ancient languages, math, physics, and astronomy. Mark was also the captain of the school's **fencing** team.

When he was a senior, Mark and another student wrote a music program called Synapse. It suggested songs to users based on what music they listened to. Large companies such as America Online (AOL) and Microsoft offered Mark more than $1 million for the program. Some companies also wanted to hire Mark full-time to write programs. However, Mark refused to sell the program and turned down the job offers.

A LOVE OF LANGUAGES

Mark can read and write in Hebrew, Latin, French, Ancient Greek, and Chinese.

CHAPTER 3

THE HARVARD YEARS

In the fall of 2002, Mark entered Harvard University in Cambridge, Massachusetts. During his sophomore year, Mark created a program called Course Match. It showed students the names of other students enrolled in a class. He also invented Facemash. This program compared pictures of Harvard students. Users voted on who was most attractive.

In February 2004, Mark and three friends created a new web site. They called it The Facebook. Users shared personal information and photos. At first, only Harvard students could sign up. However, the site was expanded because of popularity. Soon, thousands of college students from around the country were on The Facebook. Mark eventually left Harvard to focus on the site.

CHAPTER 4
THE LAUNCH OF FACEBOOK

In June 2004, Mark moved to Palo Alto, California. Other Internet companies had found success there. By the end of 2004, The Facebook had 1 million users. In 2005, Mark changed the name to just Facebook.

Mark invited the world to join Facebook in September 2006. Any teen or adult who had an email address could have an account. Facebook became a place for people to share about their lives. Businesses started to **advertise** on Facebook pages. In 2012, Facebook **shares** were sold to the public. Mark made millions of dollars from the sale. In 2013, he was worth over $19 billion!

WHY SO BLUE?
Facebook is mostly blue because Mark has red-green color blindness. He sees the color blue the best.

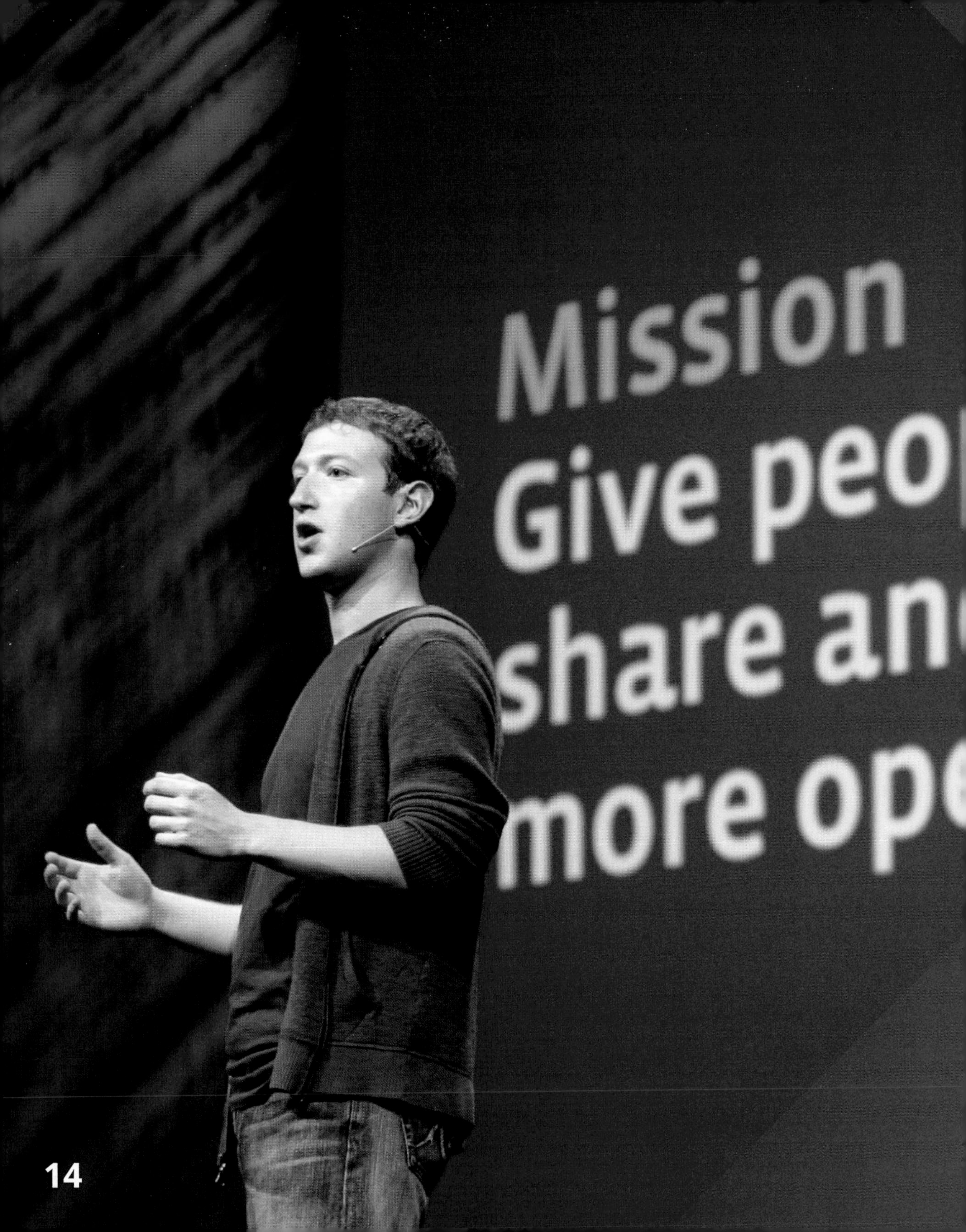
Mission

Mark achieved great success in a short time. However, he faced some problems along the way. In 2004, a few Harvard students claimed that Facebook was their idea. Mark denied their accusations. However, he agreed to pay them $65 million.

Today, some users are unhappy with Facebook. Many are concerned about their privacy. They worry that too many people and businesses have access to their personal information. Some do not agree with the values or practices of organizations that advertise on Facebook. Despite these problems, Facebook continues to grow in popularity. In 2013, Facebook had more than one billion active users.

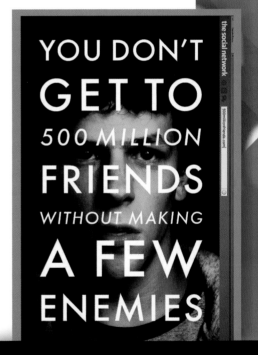

AT THE MOVIES

In 2010, the story of Mark's time at Harvard and the creation of Facebook was made into a movie. It was called *The Social Network*.

CHAPTER 5

REACHING OUT

In 2010, Mark was named Person of the Year by *Time* magazine. It chose Mark because of his huge influence on how people communicate. In May 2013, Facebook made the Fortune 500 list for the first time. This list ranks the top companies in the United States. At age 28, Mark was the youngest **CEO** on the list.

Mark is known for his generosity. In 2010, he donated $100 million to the Newark public schools in New Jersey. That year, he also signed the Giving Pledge. This is a promise to donate at least half of his wealth to charities over his

lifetime. Mark is also generous with his time. As a volunteer teacher, Mark taught business skills to middle school students in his community. The class included time at Facebook headquarters!

CHAPTER 6

FULFILLING DREAMS, TODAY AND TOMORROW

On May 19, 2012, Mark married Priscilla Chan. The two met when they were students at Harvard. Today, she is a **pediatrician**. In their spare time, Mark and Priscilla enjoy traveling to different countries. They also spend time with their Hungarian Sheepdog, Beast. The dog even has his own Facebook page and more than one million fans!

Hard work and dedication helped Mark achieve many successes at a young age. However, he still has more goals. Mark hopes that one day everyone in the world will be connected on Facebook. Many people in poor countries do not have computers. Mark is working with technology companies to bring devices to those people. He believes Facebook is meant to unite the world.

RESUME

Education

2002-2004: Harvard University (Cambridge, Massachusetts)

2000-2002: Phillips Exeter Academy (Exeter, New Hampshire)

1998-2000: Ardsley High School (Ardsley, New York)

Work Experience

2004-present: CEO and co-founder of Facebook

Community Service/Philanthropy

2013: Taught a middle school business class (East Menlo Park, California)

2013: Donated $992 million to Silicon Valley Community Foundation

2010: Donated $100 million to Newark public schools in New Jersey

LIFE TIMELINE

May 14, 1984:
Born in White Plains,
New York

Summer 2004:
Moves to Palo Alto, California,
to expand his business

Spring 2002:
Graduates from Phillips
Exeter Academy

1996:
Creates ZuckNet

Fall 2002:
Enters Harvard University

February 2004:
Launches a web site
called The Facebook

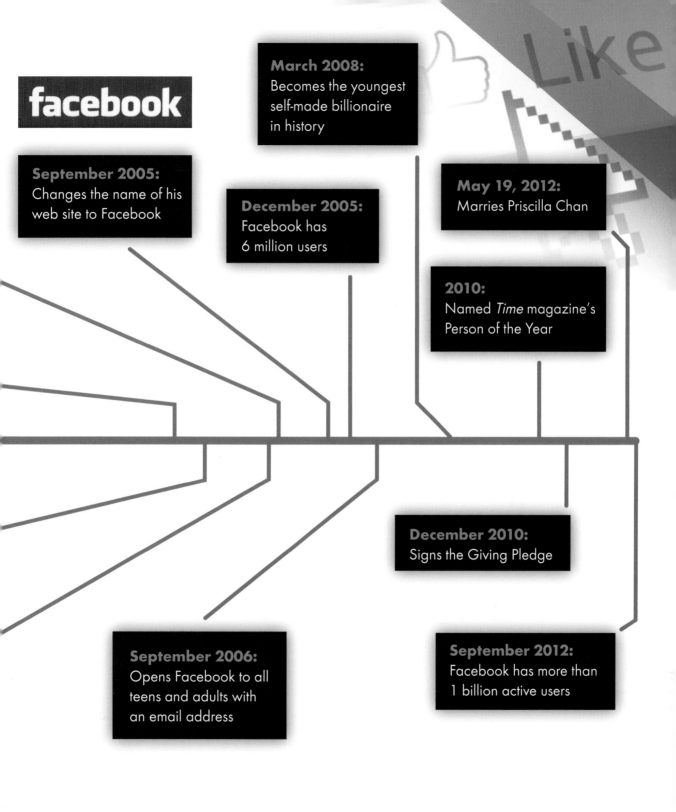

facebook

Like

March 2008:
Becomes the youngest
self-made billionaire
in history

September 2005:
Changes the name of his
web site to Facebook

December 2005:
Facebook has
6 million users

May 19, 2012:
Marries Priscilla Chan

2010:
Named *Time* magazine's
Person of the Year

December 2010:
Signs the Giving Pledge

September 2006:
Opens Facebook to all
teens and adults with
an email address

September 2012:
Facebook has more than
1 billion active users

GLOSSARY

advertise—to make the public aware of something that is being sold

CEO—Chief Executive Officer; the CEO is the highest-ranking person in a company.

co-founder—a person who founds a company with one or more people

computer code—a set of computer instructions written by a computer programmer

entrepreneur—a person who starts businesses

fencing—the sport of fighting with swords

instant messaging system—a system for chatting online with instant messages

pediatrician—a doctor who treats children

philanthropist—a person who donates money to charities and causes

prodigy—a young person who has exceptional abilities

psychiatrist—a doctor who treats people with mental illnesses

shares—units of ownership in a company

social networks—web sites and other technologies that allow users to connect with one another

TO LEARN MORE

AT THE LIBRARY

Fertig, Dennis. *Mark Zuckerberg*. Chicago, Ill.: Heinemann Library, 2013.

Goldsworthy, Steve. *Mark Zuckerberg*. New York, N.Y.: AV2 by Weigl, 2013.

Woog, Adam. *Mark Zuckerberg: Facebook Creator*. Detroit, Mich.: KidHaven Press, 2009.

ON THE WEB

Learning more about Mark Zuckerberg is as easy as 1, 2, 3.

1. Go to www.factsurfer.com.

2. Enter "Mark Zuckerberg" into the search box.

3. Click the "Surf" button and you will see a list of related web sites.

With factsurfer.com, finding more information is just a click away.

INDEX

The images in this book are reproduced through the courtesy of: Rick Friedman/ Corbis, front cover (top), p. 11; Erikona, front cover (bottom); Kimihiro Hoshino/ Newscom, pp. 4-5; Splash News/ Corbis, pp. 6, 9; Kim Kulish/ Corbis, pp. 6-7; Mike Kepka/ Corbis, pp. 8-9; Zef Nikolla/ Facebook/ Handout/ Corbis, pp. 12-13; Eric Risberg/ AP Images, pp. 14-15; A.F. Archive/ Alamy, p. 15; PR Newshire/ AP Images, p. 16; Jeff Chiu/ Corbis, pp. 16-17; Justin Sullivan/ Getty Images, p. 18; Ira Block/ Corbis, p. 20; scyther5, p. 21.